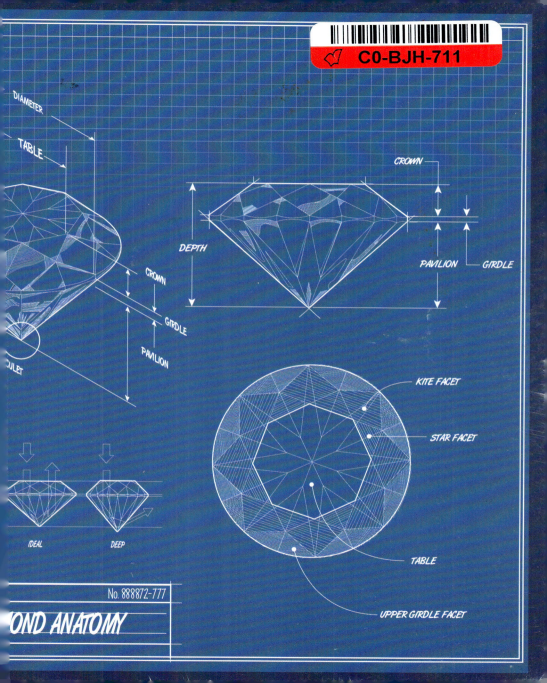

DIAMETER

TABLE

CROWN

DEPTH

CROWN

GIRDLE

PAVILION

CULET

CROWN

PAVILION

GIRDLE

KITE FACET

STAR FACET

IDEAL

DEEP

TABLE

No. 888872-777

OND ANATOMY

UPPER GIRDLE FACET

The
Guy's Guide to
Gem Buying for Girls
Otherwise Known
as the G-4 Manual

by
Dawn Dorinda Boehmer
©2009

The Guys Guide to Gem Buying
For Girls

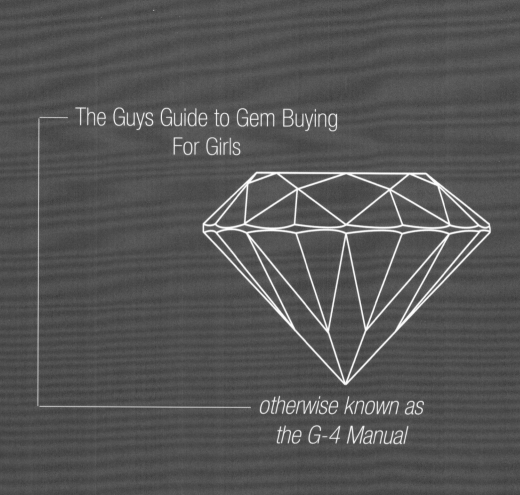

*otherwise known as
the G-4 Manual*

Introduction...................................9
The Girls......................................13
The Romantic................................17
The Modernist...............................33
The Traditionalist...........................45
Design...57
     The Romantic.....................59
     The Modernist....................67
     The Traditionalist.................75
Gems..91
Pearls...106
Metals...108
Shopping......................................112
Lists..122
Mohs Scale...................................124
Further Study.................................125
Acknowledgements..........................126
Credits...127

Table of Contents

From the dawn of time, man has agonized over one singular dilemma. Ugh, that original caveman, scratched his head over which shell to string for Ook with the same perplexity that the modern guy feels when faced with the challenge of choosing that perfect piece of jewelry for that ever so special gal. Time, technology and the advent of evolution has not made things any easier. Compared with the choices facing Modern Man, Ugh had it easy.

Introduction

Rare pieces to common pieces, there are masses of choices ... styles, colors, shapes, sizes, textures ... endless options! What's a boy to do? The risk of failure looms far above comfort level. Let's face it, it is inevitable to lose. It happens to the best of us. The trick is not to do it often. Even the Royal Jewellers to Louis XV had a blunder. Case in point: the Affair of the Queen's Necklace. Great great, great great great, great great, grandad, Charles Augustus Boehmer and his partner Bassenge had a dickens of a time selling that necklace after the untimely demise of the King. Apparently the new King, Louis the XVI and Marie Antionette weren't interested. It seemed that nary a Royal in sight was buying. Could it be true that not a single gal in all of Europe wanted the most expensive, exquisite necklace of the day? Well... 18th century or 21st, you know how picky girls can be. But don't despair, when faced with the challenges inherent with jewelry shopping, just grab your G-4 manual and practice, practice, practice.

Here's the rub, if you want to be the man who figures out what to do, you've got to put a bit of work into it. To make that a little easier, The Guys Guide to Gem Buying for Girls Otherwise Known as the G-4 Manual will provide invaluable information for your success. However, don't expect it all, there is more information out there than you could know - for that refer to page 125, Further Study. There you will find additional reading suggestions if you wish to delve further into the technical and historical aspects of gemology and jewelry craftsmanship.

The G-4 is a guide, and as a guide, the G-4 will help you; a sherpa, so to speak, to guide you through the labyrinth of jewelry shopping. But through all the twists and turns, the hunt, the appropriation and the presentation is still up to you. It is true, you know; "no guts, no glory".

Introduction

The Girls

Nary a gal around today wouldn't swoon at the sight of a beautiful bauble, presented for whatever reason. While the holidays are a perfectly safe occasion for expressing your adoration for the gal who has captured your heart, an every day, any day gift, presented in that telltale little box will always get her attention.

Yet, in the past you poor fellows were virtually left on your own to decipher through the arduous task of finding that winning piece to garner the coveted hero points gained by presenting your gal with a beautiful bauble, regardless of the occasion.

At last there is help. The G-4 will guide you through the 4 main categories every guy should know about in order to meet with success in his gem buying experience; least of which is access to a Pharaoh's sized bank vault.

The four categories are:

1. Know your girl.
2. Know your Design.
3. Know your Gems.
4. Know some technicalities.

Don't worry, the G-4 will get you through this.
And when you're done, you'll wonder why you
ever thought it was hard.

Know Your Girl

Is she Sassy or Romantic?

Modern or Traditional?

or a dizzying combination?

How do you figure it all out?

The Girls

This gentlemen, is where you have to pay attention –

and start taking notes…
(when she's not looking, of course!)

The Romantic

A true romantic is pretty easy to spot. She wears sweet feminine clothes with ruffles and lace and you may see floral patterns show up more than once. Even if she loves pants and wears a lot of black, look for the details.

Is that black top sheer with a little trim at the sleeve? Yes? Then there is clue #1

Notes:

_____

_____

_____

_____

_____

_____

_____

_____

Details on black are sometimes hard to discern. Look at the texture of the pant fabric for a clue.

Is it soft and flowing?

Are they wide legged or with a flare? This would be another clue.

Amazing how much goes into (a seemingly) simple black outfit, isn't it?

Notes:

The Romantic

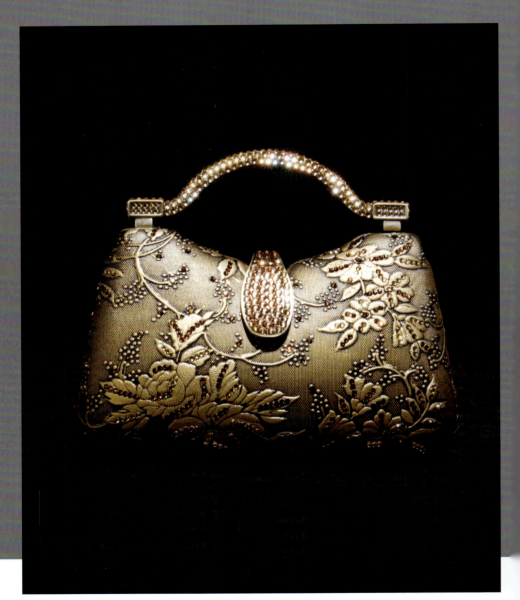

Does her handbag have extra stuff on it, a fringed clasp perhaps?

Added on appliqués or charms on the strap?

There's clue #2.

Notes:

_____

_____

_____

_____

_____

_____

_____

_____

The Romantic

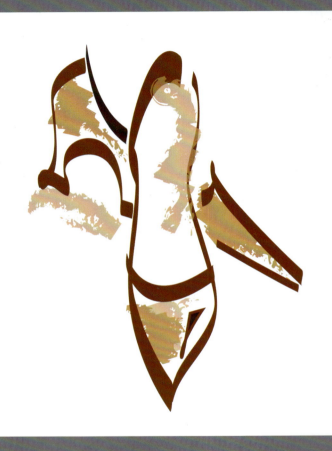

Shoes are a sure clue – are they high, medium or low heeled?

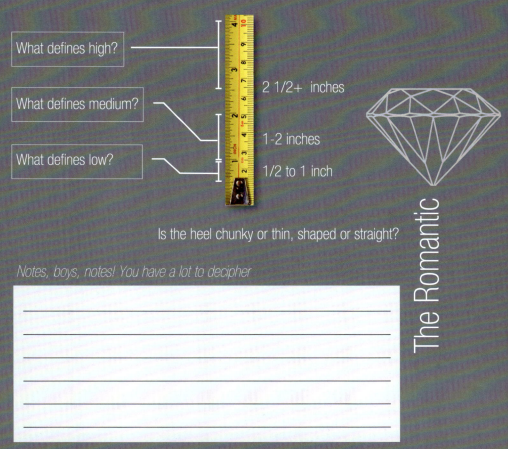

What defines high?

What defines medium?

What defines low?

2 1/2+ inches

1-2 inches

1/2 to 1 inch

Is the heel chunky or thin, shaped or straight?

Notes, boys, notes! You have a lot to decipher

The Romantic

Notes:

Notes:

_____
_____
_____
_____
_____
_____
_____
_____
_____
_____
_____
_____
_____
_____
_____
_____
_____
_____

The Romantic

Romantic gals rarely wear chunky heels, if they do, then they've fallen in love with something else about the shoe - the color, print or style – look for a super feminine element somewhere else in the design of the shoe – perhaps hot pink metallic patent leather; bows maybe … keep writing.

Notes:

or ankle ties or beaded or jeweled.
You can tell a lot about a girl by the shoes she wears!

Next pay attention to her make up.

The romantic gal will wear soft feminine and pretty colors. Not strong, yet expertly applied for maximum girl impact.

Notes:

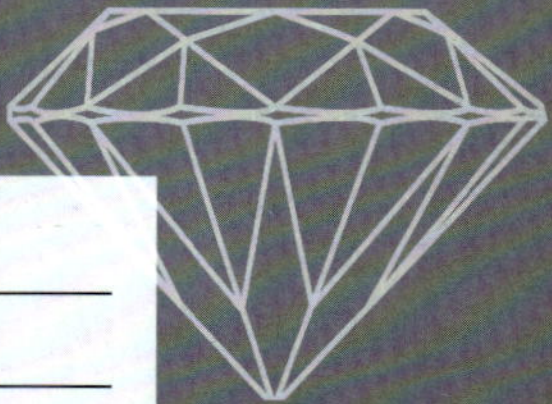

_____

_____

_____

_____

_____

_____

_____

_____

_____

Nails? check that color, does it say *"girl"* ?

The Romantic

And last but not least, does she drag you out to the latest chick flick on Friday nights?

When you're done gathering all the clues, don't be tempted to pick up on a few of the most obvious and call it a day.

Romantic gals can fall for a trendy modern piece of fashion as easily as a modern gal will blush over a romantic ruffle or two when she's in the mood.

So pay close attention before you decide.

Romantic gals have also been known by these other names: old fashioned (never!), girlie, prissie, and diva.

Such unfair name calling has never done any good.

The Romantic

The Modern Girl

A true modern gal will generally scoff at anything frilly or lacy – she is sleek, urban and, well … modern.

Ready for the no nonsense world cf urban living whether she lives in a city or not. Black is an essential wardrobe element for the modern gal but she won't be afraid of color.

Watch for sleek uncluttered pieces. You won't see lots of extra fluffiness going on with her wardrobe.

Notes:

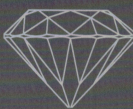

Straight skirts and tailored tops. Her sweater might just be a wrap style, no buttons to fuss with- just wrap and go! That's this gals style all the way.

Her make up is strong and bold – she will be noticed. Colors and application will be of the most current trend.

Yet, this is not to say that she isn't girlie – She presents her femininity in a more straight forward way. Opting the attitude of "no ruffles needed to tell you I'm a girl!"

Notes:

_____
_____
_____
_____
_____
_____
_____
_____
_____

The Modern Girl

Her shoes (again a key indicator) will be modern all the way — on the cutting edge of current trend.

Square toe when everyone else is wearing round. Round, when everyone else is discovering square.

Notes:

_____

_____

_____

_____

_____

_____

_____

_____

_____

_____

The Modern Girl

Notes

Notes

A modern gal is, if nothing else, an individual.

Her handbag may be from a new designer found in a downtown
boutique instead of an overworked branded label. Yet you will
notice the craftsmanship of this unknown artist to be exquisite.

Notes:

_____

_____

_____

_____

_____

_____

_____

_____

The Modern Girl

It is possible that the modern gal will follow a fashion trend with her accessories so beware that you don't mistake her for that slave to fashion: the Urbanite. This could leave irreparable damages.

How to distinguish between the two, I hear you ask –

Simple, the key difference here is that the Urbanite doesn't care about substance. As long as she's carrying the label du jour!

Therein lies the danger, assume a Modernista has no substance and she'll kick you to the curb – right after that indie flick she's drug you to has finished!

Mcdernist can also be known by these other monikers: urban, contemporary, au current, citified, and trendy.

Now, now, mind your manners.

The Modern Girl

The Traditionalist

Often the traditionalist is confused with the conservative and, mind you, many traditional gals are indeed conservative in their dress, thus, leading some gents to the wrong conclusions.

The traditionalist is more likely to pair her black skirt or pant with a crisp white tailored top or pastel colored sweater set.

Notes:

She may wear scarves a la Grace Kelly, the perfect 6mm strand of pearls and sunglasses a la Jackie O.

Notes:

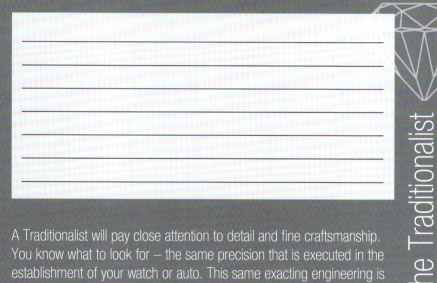

_____

_____

_____

_____

_____

_____

A Traditionalist will pay close attention to detail and fine craftsmanship. You know what to look for – the same precision that is executed in the establishment of your watch or auto. This same exacting engineering is executed in the precision construction of her handbag.

The Traditionalist

Her shoes tend to be sensible yet stylish and always appropriate for the occasion. While evening shoes may have bows or beading, these details will be delicate, feminine. They shine with the most expertly rendered bows or beads ever seen on a shoe.

Notes:

_____

_____

_____

_____

_____

_____

_____

_____

_____

The Traditionalist

She may not wear much make up at all. The minimum lipstick in a soft gentle shade may be her signature style. And chances are she'll already own her mother's pearls.

Strange as it may seem, your traditional gal won't quib a bit when you take her to all those action flicks where the hero wins every time!

Traditional gals can be known under these various pseudonyms: conservative, simple, plain (although there is nothing plain about these gals), preppie and/or yuppie.

Sticks and stones may break some bones but name calling will never hurt this gal!

The Traditionalist

Know Your Girls

Now that you've taken an attentive eye to your gal, you may have come to the realization that there is more to her than originally thought.

You also may be faced with the prospect of a combination gal. If that's the case a little more research will be needed to understand her true essence.

Essence, after all boys, is what we are after to truly understand our women.

Why so much fuss just to buy some trinkets. You are so brave to ask-

Because jewelry, my good man, is the reflection of the essence of a woman.

And if you don't get it right, well … you'll get it wrong.

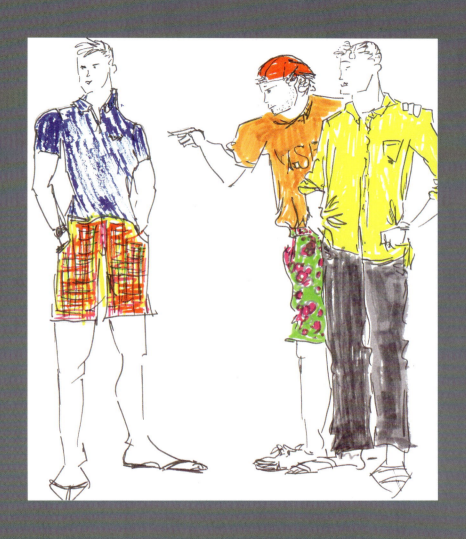

What makes it **Romantic?**

What makes it **Modern?**

What makes it **Traditional?**

Deciphering Design

Not an easy task by any means. Design is such an all encompassing topic that to keep it somewhat simple is truly a herculean task.

To make it a little easier, I'll draw some analogies to things which you may be more familiar:

Cars,
Dogs, *and*
Architecture

I know it sounds odd, but trust me, it will soon make sense ...

Design

Victorian style Architecture

a Borzoi

Zeisels' style curvilinear coffee table.

The Romantic

Imagine your gal zipping down the street in her BMW M3 convertible (did I mention that it was red?).

She pulls into the driveway of her multi color Victorian with a full wrap around porch.

She is greeted by her sleek coated Borzoi (or perfectly coiffed Pekinese pups), awaiting patiently in her own lushly upholstered, curve legged doggie daybed, which is strategically located near the thick velvet window coverings and next to a Zeisel style table.

Sound familiar? Then you've found a true romantic.

Design: Romantic

Lavish attention is poured out on to all who come into the romantics' sphere. Care and consideration are never overlooked- indicated by that lush treatment of her pets!

How does this translate into jewelry?

When choosing gems for this gal, keep a keen eye on all things luxurious.

The care and attention you spend on your purchase needs to be obvious. How to make something obvious when it is a surprise?
A bit of a paradox you say?

Here's the rub - If it fits her personality exactly, she'll know that you're paying attention to *her*. This, my man, is your key to success.

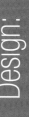

Design: Romantic

Suppose your gal isn't quite a true blue romantic, perhaps she is a bit more subtle. How would you know the difference?

Imagine this:

Your gal is zipping down the street in her Range Rover, British Racing Green that is, she pulls into the drive of her two tone Victorian with a small entry porch.

Bounding impatiently from the doggie door, bolts her Rhodesian Ridgeback, fresh from her nap on the plump and cozy bay window cushions.

The two seem at first glance to be quite dissimilar. But, upon closer inspection you'll see the parallels.

Design: Romantic

Honestly, what could be more romantic than an African Safari holiday or for those who aren't crazy about the realities of 13 foot tall ant hills, a rainy night in curled up watching *Out of Africa*?

And what vehicle of comfort is the auto de rigueur for said terrain of safari but the Range Rover. The poetic conclusion to such a romantic getaway would surely be to bring home a Ridgeback pup and name her Inga.

Sheer romance at every turn!

Design: Romantic

The Modernist

True to her modernists beat, this gal will be inspired by all things new, contemporary, and individualistic.

You're likely to find your Modern gal garaging her prized Porche or coveted high gloss black Masserati Coupe in the comfort of her Frank Lloyd Wright inspired (if not authentic) abode.

Design: Modern

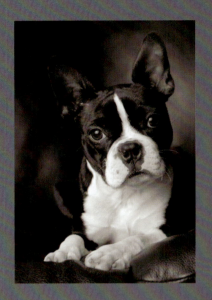

Filled with Mies van der Rohe furnishings and a custom Courbusier doggie day bed for her Boston Terrier named Bruce.

How does this translate into jewelry? When choosing gems for this gal search for the unique unusual things that have an out-side the box esthetic. Unique and interesting pieces are easily found at craft/art shows. Pieces called "jewelers follies" are one of a kind pieces that independent craftsmen have created as artistic expressions.

Design: Modern

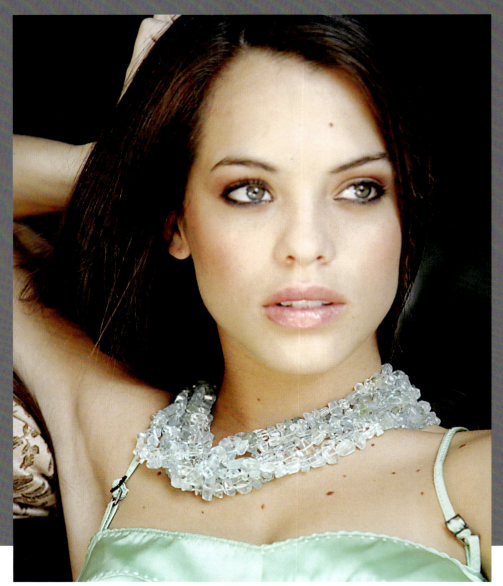

Modern gals will also find amusement in the quirky, giving you lots more freedom in your range of jewelry choices.

But think carefully about bringing home an ordinary strand of beads to your modern gal, find something extraordinary about that strand of beads or reconsider your choice.

A modern gal wearing jewelry out of obligation is worse than a fish out of water. They both tend to get a little stinky!

Design: Modern

Suppose your gal is a modernist in the making...

The modern gal on a budget is equally as esoteric, so don't be fooled by her mild mannered modernism. She might sport about in her vintage Saab or that shiny Blue Mini Cooper, but that standard Poodle, named Auri, seated in the front seat really does have that haughty aire of his namesake Marcus Aurelius.

Look past the old Bauhaus furnishings from mom and dad's basement that fill her condo.

Until that promotion comes through, she'll make the best of it ... with a little help from Ikea.

Design: Modern

The Traditionalist

Sporting a Buick or perhaps that Caddy STS, you'll find your traditional gal zipping down the street in her exactingly engineered performance auto. High on performance and dependability, pristine engineering is just her thing.

Her dependability streak is by no means a disadvantage. Function over form may be her mantra but who among you dare question the performance factor of that Cadillac?

Design: Traditional

At home, blithely tall potted topiary grace the foyer while sectional furniture finds contented domestic bliss in her efficient townhouse. Spiced up with exacting balance is an Arco floor lamp, the function here actually provides the comfort – what logic!

To keep a discerning eye on the lair, her indomitable Doberman Pincher; guarding dutifully.

Design: Traditional

The discerning eye of the traditionalist narrows considerably the choices that will make her smile. Not a bad thing, sometimes too many choices can cause you to be indecisive. Never an envious position to be in when it comes to jewelry shopping. Stay focused, stay decisive and stay close to … tradition. Nothing frivolous will most appeal. The gems need to stand on their own. A single strand of lustrous pearls. A solitaire gem with exceptional brilliance and color. These are a few of her favorite things.

With the exacting eye of a traditionalist, finding pieces for her on a budget may be a bit of a challenge. Just think performance, your traditional gal will be much happier with lesser valued gems of superior quality, then valuable gems of no quality.

Rings with no bling – bring no smiles.

Design: Traditional

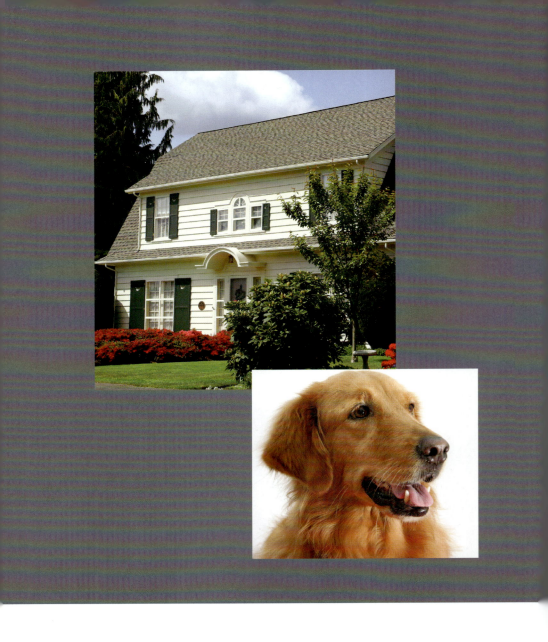

The tepid traditionalist maybe sporting about in a Volvo full of dog hair, but don't be fooled by that seemingly laissez-faire attitude. This gal still loves her organized life, she just loves her Golden Retriever more than she hates the fur covered back seat.

Although the plumbing in that restored colonial might be a bit temperamental, your tepid traditionalist rarely is. Shabby chic furniture may distract you in to thinking that your gal is more bohemian than most, again don't be fooled.

Designed for ultimate in comfort, this gal's eye knows a performance buster when she sees it.

Design: Traditional

So, how does all this information translate in jewelry and gem buying you ask? Good Question.

The G-4 will show you — Read on.

Design: Traditional

The Romantic

Possibly the easiest style to shop for, the romantic loves anything super feminine.

Curly Q's and bows, floral and vintage styling. All things that look lacy and earrings that sway when she moves. Gems with romantic folklore will also appeal to your romantic gal (more on folklore in the gem chapter).

Design

The Modernist

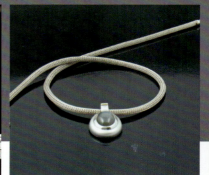

She'll love all things new and exciting, things that push the boundaries and defy physics.

Look for pieces with a decidedly sculptural and architectural edge.

An eclectic mix will also appeal to her highly individualized personality.

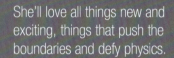

Design

The Traditionalist

Last but not least, your traditional gal. Some say that
she is easier to shop for than the romantic.

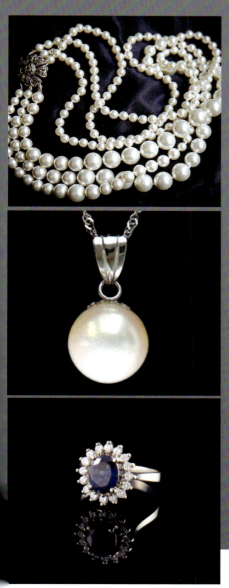

Look for things that are familiar, symmetrical in balance and color. Remember, subtlety is your best focus. Matched sets are always a bonus.

Design

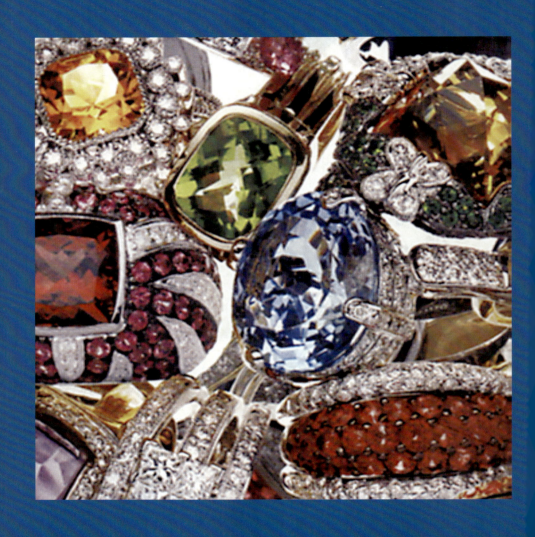

Gems

Now that you have a grasp of who your gal is, what designs are most likely to appeal to her and how this would translate into jewelry design, we can delve into the more comprehensive technical realm of gems. Their characteristics, personalities and the folklore surrounding them that has been carried down for generations upon generations.

Hidden deep within the earth's surface there are gorgeous gems just waiting to be found.

We use to wait for volcanic eruption to spit them out or weather erosion to reveal their hiding places. Luckily for us, the Industrial Age brought with it machinery that could dig and dig and dig. So you see, the nickname "rock" isn't such a reach.

All those beautiful gems, sparkling under the jewelry case lights, started out as a simple and unassuming rock. Through the process of faceting and polishing a beautiful jewel emerges.

Gems come in all colors and mineral compositions and are categorized in familial groups- like bugs, or cars; A Shelby Cobra is to the Ford family as an Amethyst is to the Quartz family.

There is a plethora of beautiful gem stones available for you to dazzle your gal.
And for girls ... it's all about the pretty ... and the romance.

Quartz, with a chemical composition of $SiO2$ ... let's skip the boring stuff and get right to the romance. Believed by the Greeks and ancient Romans to be ice that had never melted because it was formed by the Gods. They kept large specimens of quartz in their atria to cool their hands on hot days.

Well, that's great for the ancient Greeks, but how, you may ask, will that translate to romance for your very current gal?

Ah, she cools your burning heart.

Amethyst is loved for its color, rich royal purple. Yet those ancient Greeks believed its color came from the tears of Dionysus, God of wine and revelry. Thus the belief that Amethyst prevented drunkenness.

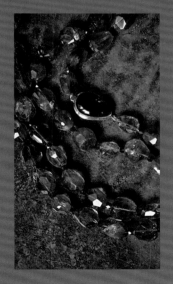

How do you romance that! I hear you scoff...

um......she is intoxicating! and the Queen of your heart!

Next up is the Citrine - that gorgeous yellow color is as bright as the sun!

Too easy, fellows — she lights up your world.

Gems

Opal (milky white), Fire Opal (orangey red), and Boulder Opal (bright blues). Worn by Pliny the Elder (AD 23-79), the Roman scholar and naturalist, his fascination with this multi hued stone is legendary. Loved by the ancient Aztecs, used in Middle Ages, celebrated by Shakespeare and a favorite of Queen Victoria and my grandmother. It is said to have the ability to awaken psychic powers. Thank goodness that wasn't the case with Gran.

One word of caution: Opal can contain up to 10% water, if it dries out (at the mining stage or after a few generations) it will crack. Therefore, it has a definitively undeserved superstition of bad luck attached to it.

The romance ... Opalios is the Greek name for Opal meaning 'precious stone'. She is your 'precious', isn't she?

Aquamarine: Latin for sea water.

Thus lending enormous amounts of seaworthy tales to it's folklore. Known as treasure from mermaids, sailors used this gem as a good luck charm.

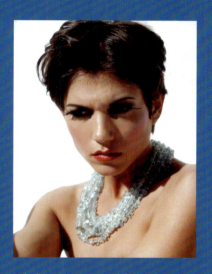

Gems

The romance – Is it not your good fortune to have such a beautiful and lovely lady in your life?

The blue is of unsurpassed beauty, especially if they match her eyes – a pair of earrings and you'll be a hero for a very long time!

Sapphire has been worn and adored since the early days of 800 BC. This gem so captivated the imagination of the ancient Persians that they believed that the sky was merely its reflection.

Sapphire has also been worn as a talisman to ward off illness, and as protection while traveling.

The romance: To present your gal with a Sapphire is to acknowledge that she has you completely and totally captivated.

In antiquity, Ruby was known as the king of gems; a gem more highly prized than diamonds. The use of ruby in ornamentation has been recorded in the Bible. Ancient records indicate that ruby mining was in full swing since the sixth century AD.

Worn as talisman to protect against illness and misfortune. Wait, you say, isn't that the same folklore as a sapphire? Yes, it is – because ruby is simply a red sapphire!

What makes the sapphire red is an exposure to chromium; which is pretty rare, just like your gal.

There is much more folklore surrounding this precious gem. And it is in the folklore, my good man, where one finds the romance.

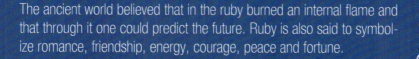

The ancient world believed that in the ruby burned an internal flame and that through it one could predict the future. Ruby is also said to symbolize romance, friendship, energy, courage, peace and fortune.

The romance: By now you should be quite adept at this. Somehow, I think what ever you choose to say, if it is said with the intensity of a pure heart, your gal is sure to swoon.

Gems

Emeralds are popular and have been for millennia —

Their lush green color has captivated us as far back as 3000
BC when the Egyptians were known to have mined this gem at
Cleopatra's Mines.

Long associated with the Roman Goddes Venus, Emerald's folklore
centers on spring, rebirth and love.

The romance?
By now you guys should be ahead of me — She is your Venus, non?

And last but not least, the Diamond.

Volumes upon volumes of material have been written about the diamond. There are those that spend entire lifetimes in the study of this jewel.

So, if you are going to get your gal a diamond- if you are ready for that step – because no matter what other type of jewelry you buy her besides the ring, the diamond will send a definite message of love and commitment from you.

Do your homework.

There are 4 major considerations to finding a quality diamond for you to familiarize yourself with prior to going into a jewelry store or speaking with your jeweler. They are: Cut, Clarity, Color and Carat weight (and not necessarily in that order). The combination of all 4 of these characteristics will determine the price you will pay for the stone.

Gems

The first thing to consider is Cut. If the proportions of the cut are not accurately executed, the light will either "fall out" of the bottom (known as the pavilion), or "leak out" of the sides of the pavilion – the correct cut will insure that the most light bounces back to the eye with the max amount of bling (known as fire or scintillation).

Diamonds can also be cut into fancy shapes.

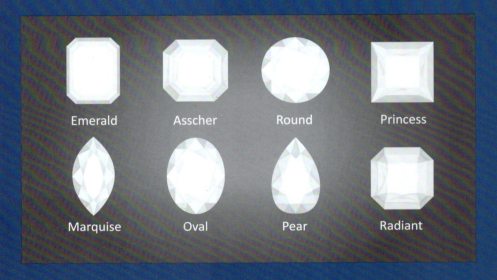

Emerald   Asscher   Round   Princess

Marquise   Oval   Pear   Radiant

Some gals are very particular about which shapes they like and which they don't. Make sure you know.

Round is the most popular. It is handy to know that one will always find maximum performance from a round (also known as brilliant) cut gem. After all, it is all about the bling.

Gems

In my opinion the next consideration is Clarity — A LOT of folks will argue with me that Color is more important — to them I say, "Phish!". I'll sacrafice color for clarity anyday.

And here is why...

As you know, diamonds are suppose to be very sparkle-y — this is called "clean". This comes from the capacity of carbon to bend the white light into the full spectrum. Yes, good quality diamonds will "throw" a rainbow of color across the room when asked nicely.

Now, here's the rub — being compressed carbon comes with inherent blemishes, imperfections that are found in the interior of the jewel that are referred to as "inclusions". The fewer the inclusions, the "cleaner" the stone and the higher the price.

Why? because inclusions absorb and/or stop light. Hence, less light bouncing back to the eye in the form of bling (aka fire).

There is a grading system for this:

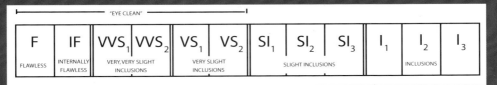

Next up, Color - Since diamonds occur in all the colors of the spectrum, there is a grading system for this as well. Colorless being the start, and grading out to black (yes, there really are black diamonds):

Gems

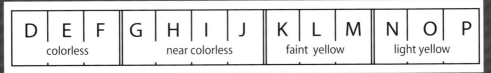

and so on.

I certainly would not say no to a mesmerizing Canary(yellow), or a precious pink, nor would I say no to a brilliant blue or any of the other colors for that matter.

But, some gals want only the white of what they understand a diamond should be. In that case, get as close to what is known as "eye clean" as possible for your budget. Eye clean means that one can not see any inclusions to the naked eye. Meaning, with out a jewelers loupe- which is a hand held 10 power magnifying glass.

If you are not ready to present your gal with a diamond, but she loves sparkle, consider the jewel Moissanite. Moissanite is not a "fake diamond" as so many mistake.

THE LOUPE

Moissanite is the jewel name for silicone carbide (SiC). It is found in meteorites and in kimberlite veins (the same place where diamonds are found), Moissanite is too tiny in its natural state to facet. Technology has given us the capability to culture this rare and beautiful gem (like pearls). Thus, large enough jewels can now be faceted and set in jewelry. And with twice the fire of a diamond, who can resist?

But why would they bother? I hear you ask.

You mean to tell me that we've gotten to the end of this chapter on gems and you still can't see that glaring opportunity for romance staring you straight in the eye?

Gems

Moissanite comes from the heavens. Isn't your gal an angel from heaven?

Better yet, if you're ready, give her diamonds and Moissanite. When was the last time you gave your gal the heavens and the earth?

Pearls

Most of us know, at least, that pearls come from oysters — well, mollusks, actually. But beyond that things get a little hazy. The G-4 is here to help clear things up.

Yes, mollusks produce pearls naturally when a grain of something irritating manages to lodge itself inside the shell. Which is pretty rare considering how tightly sealed those creatures are. Not to be undone the mollusks sets to work coating a gazillion layers of protective mucus, called nacre, around this irritation. When it stops irritating the mollusk stops working and returns to his previously blissful existence.

Along comes a hungry man, cracks open his dinner and is surprised by something wonderful, lustrous and beautiful. A new challenge ensues: how to find more. The search is on.

Until one day, Kokichi Mikimoto found a better way. Why search when one can create? In 1893, Mikimoto's research and diligence paid off and he was rewarded with a pearl.

Pearls can be cultured in freshwater or salt depending upon the desired outcome. Cultured freshwater pearls are less uniform in shape (some gals prefer this) and generally less expensive. The layers of nacre are what give the pearl luster. More luster, more expense.

Pearls can be under a hundred dollars or well into six figures, so here is some insider info on why that is – Mikimoto Pearls are the most expensive because they use a pearl irritant to grow a new pearl. These pearls have a more intense luster than any other cultured pearl. Some mass marketed pearls actually start with a plastic bead – these will be the least expensive of your choices because these pearls have fewer layers of nacre.

Pearls

Be prepared to hear some flack over the "cultured/created" debate – ie: " the oyster made it". Yes, but Mr. Oyster wouldn't have unless man threw the "on" switch! We'd be waiting for ever if it was up to the oyster and we're too impatient for that. Our girls love their pearls too much to wait around for Mr. Mollusk to do this on his own.

I know you're just dying to get out there and conquer the world, but there is just one more bit of infcrmation that will come in handy...

KNOW YOUR METALS

GOLD

You may be familiar with icons that look similar to this: 10K, 14K, 18K

These hallmarks, as they are known in the industry, indicate the amount of gold in the alloy that is used to create jewelry.

Pure gold (24K) is too scft – also known as malleable – for jewelry so other metals are added to it to produce an alloy. The hallmark indicates the amount of gold in the mix.

Here's the breakdown:

10K contains 41.6% gold, 14K contains 58.5% gold and 18K contains 75%.

The price is reflected in the carat weight and is directly correlated to the price of gold on current trading markets.

It was at the end of WWII that this hallmark was required on all finished jewelry. Look for it on rings inside the ring itself. For necklaces, look on or near the clasp. Earrings are difficult because of their small size, but look on the bottom of the basket or near the post.

To watch your budget, watch the markets. By knowing the current market price for gold, you will be able to determine whether the retail price for a piece is fair. If it sounds too cheap - it might not be what it is pretending to be.

SILVER

A word on silver – utilized for several millenia by jewelers and silversmiths to create beautiful and functional pieces throughout history. Clasps of silver used to secure clothing were the standard long before the invention of snaps, pins or zippers!

Silver for jewelry is usually with mixed copper for strength, the alloy must be at least 92.5% silver in order to carry the hallmark 925 to be sold as 925 sterling.

So, don't forget to look for the 925 hallmark before you purchase.

Also silver will tarnish, which is okay as it cleans up relatively easy. To get a high glossy polished look, jewelers will coat the silver in an alloy called rhodium.

Metals

Rhodium will also be plated onto other metals. The most popular being platinum and white gold.

Platinum has been used for jewelry more frequently since jewelers learned to work with this rare metal around 1900.

Often 3 times more expensive than gold, platinum is a discerning choice for jewelry when the budget allows.

Platinum has a matte like pewter appearance, and similar to white gold, has a rhodium finish to give it shine.

White gold, as most are unaware, is an alloy mix of gold and other light colored metals; as there is no natural white gold. It is always plated in rhoduim to give it it's shine.

Rhodium will wear away upon constant contact with the skin- this is due to the reaction to the wearers Ph balance. Thus, white gold and platinum will require periodic maintenance to re-coat the rhodium and keep the piece shiny and new in appearance.

You are now armed with enough knowledge to go shopping.

Metals

Wait! One more thing before you go...

Let's talk dollars.

Shopping

Top dog in gem buying for girls is undisputedly Sir Richard Burton. The man knew. He had a flare for the dramatic, an eye for beauty, and the fat cat wallet to make it all happen.

Don't worry boys, you don't have to be Mr. Burton to pick up a treat now and again for your gal. The G-4 manual will guide you through the arduous task of finding the winning piece without breaking the bank.

While access to a Burton sized checkbook would certainly make things easier, dollars don't always equal success in this game.

It really is best to plan your budget before you go shopping. This way you avoid the costly up-sell. Your budget should start at 200 dollars, but if you must do on less, the G-4 is here to help.

So, you've got Ten Bucks, maybe 20 – honestly you won't go far with that scrawny a budget – but, if that's it then that's it.

$10

Your best chance of appropriating any sort of anything that resembles jewelry is to go to a major department store and check out the clearance racks. Look for silver. You may get lucky.

Note here on 'silver tone'. Silver tone is a mixed alloy with a shiny silver finish, to look like silver – it won't last and may even turn her skin green.

If there is nothing in silver, perhaps a charm on a leather strap will do. Or a wooden bangle, or maybe something funky in papier maché or beads.

Although ten to twenty bucks isn't the ideal budget to impress your girl, don't despair. Savvy shopping with ten will impress her a whole lot more than a thoughtless toss at twenty. Which is exactly what she'll do; as soon as your back is turned!

Shopping

$50

So you've got a fifty, what's a guy to do? This much might get you off the clearance racks and onto the sale racks; maybe. Again, stay away from the silver tone – She buys tons of her own silver tone, she doesn't really need any more from you, budget or no budget. Unless it is so perfect that you can present that necklace, bracelet, whatever with the following iron clad disclaimer:

"It won't last forever, hon, but is so perfect with that new…
(fill in the blank)   that you bought last week that I just couldn't resist."

Not up to that - then don't even go there.

Honestly to find something worth your effort, something that says romance, you'll need at least 100 bucks.

$100

Mind you, this still leaves you at the sale counter, but a least you'll be able to find a nice pair of Amethyst earrings or a pendent in blue Topaz or Citrine. You will be looking at 10K gold. But if there's a good sale running you may be able to find something in 14K.

One hundred should buy you a nice piece of turquoise, jade, or a strand of pearls.

The two to five hundred dollar range really opens things up for you. Your choices will be much broader here and your shopping venues will expand as well. You can now move out of the department store sale counter and bargain bin and saunter over to the glass cases.

Shopping

$500

You will find many of the same jewels, yet there will be something different about them. A bit more substantial, you say? Um, yes, and more varied. These pieces will have more or larger jewels. There will be an obvious amount of craftsmanship apparent with the piece. And you will find in this budget bracket the start of Brand names.

Often, the amount of choice is not necessarily a good thing, you'll want to stay focused because it is at this point where one can easily be distracted with all the options.

From 500 to One Thousand, the possibilities are even greater. This budget really opens up the market for you.
A beautiful pair of gold hoops, a gold chain or bracelet - for all those charms you'll be getting later on. A sexy pair of chandelier earrings, or some bangles – one for each year you've been together, or each time she made you smile.

Honestly, do you think I'd forget about romance, just because we're talking about money?   tsck tsck.

$1000

A grand and up? Maybe half a mil? Well, now you're talking. This budget opens you up to a whole new world. Brand names big and small just awaiting your arrival through big name doors to big name stores — think Neiman Marcus, Tiffany's, etcetera — It also puts you in the 18K range.

A quick word about 18K, if someone tries to tell you that the piece is 18K and it is not considerably more expensive than a 14K piece, then something isn't right.

And by now gentlemen, you should be savvy to that.

The price for white or yellow gold should be relatively the same. Some folks have been known to charge a bit more for white gold because of the rhodium plating. The difference should be nominal; if anything.

Shopping

This budget also puts you in diamond and fine quality gemstone range. Although you can purchase diamonds well below the thousand dollar range, you may want to consider whether or not you really want to.

Diamonds that are in the, I1,2, or 3 clarity category maybe less expensive, but you will find no brilliance, no fire, no life. Nothing of what a diamond is about. There are so many other options, why would you want to waste any dollars at all on a diamond that, well, isn't really worth it. Better a gorgeous opal than an opal-like diamond!

In my personal opinion.

Shopping

Up you walk to that counter; there it is in all its glory, sparkling brighter than a solar eclipse. Over slides a silver tongued sales associate, ready, willing and able to separate you from your money...

It felt that way, didn't it, before the G-4.

Now, it is different.

Now, you are ready and able to make your own decisions, based on knowledge and facts.

Shop with the confidence and pride we know is in you - let no clerk dissuade you from your rightful purchase!

Now you are the master of your own jewelry shopping destiny!!

Go forth man and conquer!

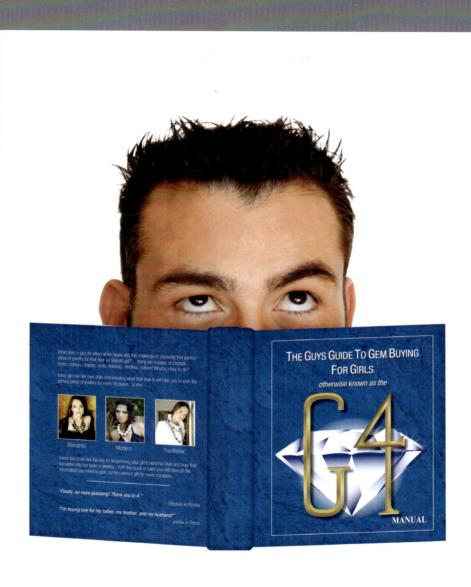

THE GUYS GUIDE TO GEM BUYING
FOR GIRLS

otherwise known as the

G4

MANUAL

What does a guy do when when faced with the challenge of choosing that perfect piece of jewelry for that ever so special gal? ... there are masses of choices, styles, colours, shapes, sizes, textures... endless options! What's a boy to do?

Every girl has her own style and knowing what that style is will help you to pick the perfect piece of jewelry for every occasion. Is she...

Romantic   Modern   Traditional

Inside this book lies the key to deciphering your girl's personal style and how that translates into her taste in jewelry. With this book in hand you will have all the information you need to pick out the perfect gift for every occasion.

"Finally, no more guessing! Thank you G-4."

Stephen in Florida

"I'm buying one for my father, my brother, and my husband!"

Joanie in Texas

Lists

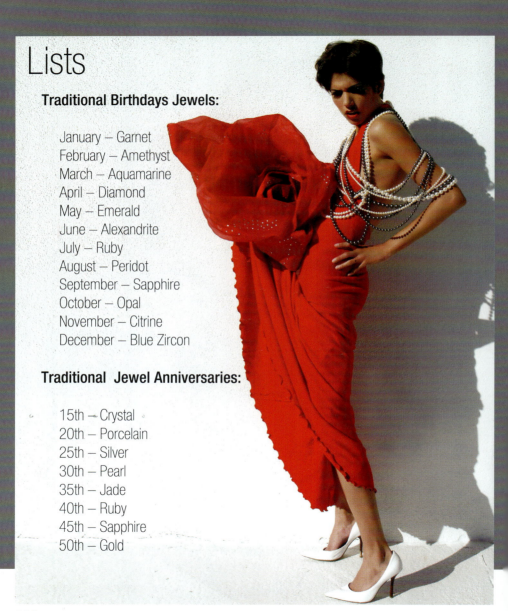

Traditional Birthdays Jewels:

January – Garnet
February – Amethyst
March – Aquamarine
April – Diamond
May – Emerald
June – Alexandrite
July – Ruby
August – Peridot
September – Sapphire
October – Opal
November – Citrine
December – Blue Zircon

Traditional Jewel Anniversaries:

15th – Crystal
20th – Porcelain
25th – Silver
30th – Pearl
35th – Jade
40th – Ruby
45th – Sapphire
50th – Gold

Lists

Zodiac Gems:

Aquarius, January 20 to February 18 – Garnet
Pisces, February 19 to March 21 – Amethyst, Aquamarine
Aries, March 22 to April 19 – Bloodstone
Taurus, April 20 to May 20 – Sapphire
Cancer, June 22 to July 22 – Emerald
Leo, July 23 to August 22 – Peridot, Onyx
Virgo, August 23 to September 22 – Carnelian
Libra, September 23 to October 23 – Opal
Scorpio, October 24 to November 21 – Beryl
Sagittarius, November 22 to December 21 – Topaz
Capricorn, December 22 to January 19 – Ruby

There are even designated gems for the days of the week!

Monday – Pearl, Feldspar
Tuesday – Star Sapphire, Ruby, Emerald
Wednesday – Amethyst, Star Ruby
Thursday – Sapphire, Carnelian
Friday – Cat's Eye, Alexandrite
Saturday – Turquoise
Sunday – Diamond

Seasonal Gems:

Winter – Diamond   Spring – Emerald   Summer – Ruby

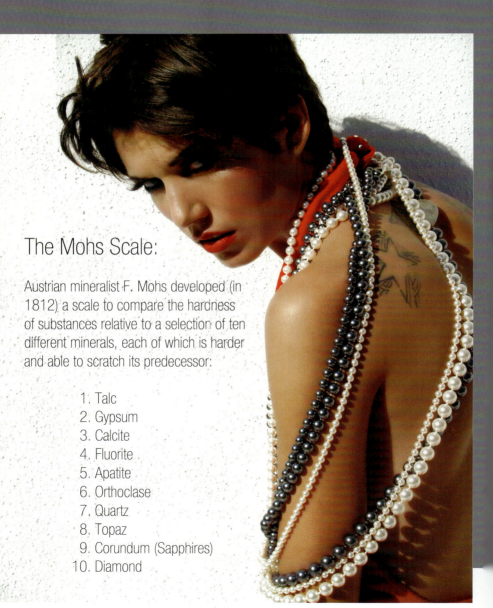

The Mohs Scale:

Austrian mineralist F. Mohs developed (in 1812) a scale to compare the hardness of substances relative to a selection of ten different minerals, each of which is harder and able to scratch its predecessor:

1. Talc
2. Gypsum
3. Calcite
4. Fluorite
5. Apatite
6. Orthoclase
7. Quartz
8. Topaz
9. Corundum (Sapphires)
10. Diamond

Further Study

The possibilities for indepth study on Gems and gemology are endless. However, here are a few options to get you started:

The Diamond Coach by Gary Ptak – *www.garyptak.com*
The Diamonds of Tiffany by Harry N. Abrams – *www.abramsbooks.com*
Diamond Buying Guide (an e-book) by Gary Ptak – *www.garyptak.com*
The National Gem Collection by Dr. Jeffery Post – *www.abramsbooks.com*
The Guide to Gems by Cally Oldershaw, published by Firefly Books, sold at your
    local booksellers, ISBN # 13:978-1-55297-814-6.
A Guide To Crystals by Jennie Harding, published by Parragon Books,
        ISBN# 0-75257-782-4
The Smithsonian Institute/ Museum of Natural History – *www.mnh.si.edu*
Pearls - *www.mikimotoamerica.com/history/index.html*

and for general sites of interest:
    www.alexandrite.net
    www.gia.org
    www.gemstone.org

Anniversaries: *www.bernardine.com/jewelry-anniv.htm*

For shopping:
    www.multicolor.com   *www.tiffany.com*
    www.barney.com   *www.rubylane.com*
    www.felissimo.com

Acknowledgments:

I would be remiss if I didn't acknowledge all those in my life that have given me love, kindness, affection and assistance along life's path. There have been many; some know exactly what they have contributed and others have no awareness that their generous unconditional kindness has had an impact on my life. To all of you I say, with deepest sincerity, Thank you.

Natalie Melissa Thurston and Grey Wardell, Timothy Scott, Zachary and Ian Thurston. Elisabeth Farchette, Victoria Bowman and Robert Rosario, Michael Sarnacchiaro, Cynthia Ngai, Mimi Jackson. Sonal Mehta, Dijana Prusac, Jennifer Raley and Lori Ballard and Elpida Parnel, David Rhodes and Greg Nagengast, Andrew and "Bones" Costello, Miss Carol Fox, Leslie McCray, Amy Boehmer Gil and Charles F. Boehmer III, Joan Potter, Ellin Wall and Keeley Boehmer. Sherrie Leavens, Mary Harding Ross, James G. McGibbon Jr., "London" and Lesly LaRoche, Lorraine Schimmenti and Dina Salem. Jershon and Carina Egar, Christian and Annie Juttner, and Karen Viviers. To my Lord Jesus Christ and to the musicians who have soothed me, inspired me and motivated me during this project: Dulce Pontes, Josh Grobin, Wolfgang Amadeus Mozart, Johann Sebastian Bach, and Antonio Lucio Vivaldi.

Credits

Jewelry Designer: Karen Viviers — *www.karenviviers.com*
Dress Designer: Sylvio — *www.SlyioKovacic.com*
Models:
- Cheryl (Alexa Models)
- Christiana
- Crystal (Benz Models)
- Kelli (Level Models)
- Nanaliz Muntean
- Natalia
- Soliel Case
- Taraneh Cocco

Photographers:
- Shamayim — *www.Shamayim.net*
- Susan Jeffers — *www.susanjeffersphotography.com*
- Jorge Alvarez — *jorge@alvarezphoto.com*

Makeup Artist:
- Brenda C. — *www.Brendacolon.com*

Hair Stylist:
- Luisa V. — *www.LuisaV.com*

Illustrations:
- Debbie Tuzel — *www.artofdesignid.com*
- New Light Design Studio — *www.newlightdesignstudio.i8.com*

Stock Photography:
- *www.istockphoto.com*

About the Author

A two hundred year old genome planted firmly in the authors' psyche caused an irrepressible love of jewelry to plague her throughout her life. From the tender age of three she has been collecting rocks. She still does; just these days they have more bling.

An equally irrepressible urge to remove the anxiety of jewelry shopping and fill the reader with confidence, has caused her to write this book.

And if you're wondering: she has grown up to become a traditionally romantic Modernista.